Little Stars

Little Stars
BALLET

A CRABTREE SEEDLINGS BOOK

Taylor Farley

CRABTREE
PUBLISHING COMPANY
WWW.CRABTREEBOOKS.COM

It's Saturday!
We have **ballet** class.

I wear a **leotard** and ballet shoes.

5

We use a **barre** for our warm-up exercises.

We practice our **positions**.

First position

Heels touching, toes turned out.

Second position

Feet apart, arms wide open.

Third position

* One foot in front of the other, touching.

Fourth position

One foot in front of the other, with a space between them.

Fifth position

No space between your feet.
Both arms up in an **oval**.

15

Our ballet teacher expects us to do our best.

When I am older, I will wear **pointe shoes**.

We love ballet!

Glossary

ballet (BAL-lay): Ballet is a style of dance.

barre (BAR): A barre is a handrail attached to the wall. Ballet dancers use a barre for training and exercises.

leotard (LEE-uh-tard): A leotard is a tight, stretchy piece of clothing worn for exercise or dancing.

oval (OH-vuhl): An oval has a long, round shape like an egg.

pointe shoes (POYNT SHOOZ):
Ballet dancers wear pointe shoes
so they can stand on the tips of
their toes.

positions (puh ZISH unz):
Positions are ways to pose your
body.

Index

23

School-to-Home Support for Caregivers and Teachers

Crabtree Seedlings books help children grow by letting them practice reading. Here are a few guiding questions to help the reader build his or her comprehension skills. Possible answers are included.

Before Reading

- **What do I think this book is about?** I think this book is about ballet dancing. It might tell us about how children learn ballet.

- **What do I want to learn about this topic?** I want to learn about different ballet moves. I also wonder what clothing ballet dancers wear.

During Reading

- **I wonder why...** I wonder why ballet dancers do warm-up exercises.

- **What have I learned so far?** I learned that there are five ballet positions. I also learned that dancers wear leotards and ballet shoes.

After Reading

- **What details did I learn about this topic?** I learned that ballet dancers must practice a lot. They take classes with ballet teachers.

- **Write down unfamiliar words and ask questions to help understand their meaning.** I see the word *leotard* on page 4 and the word *barre* on page 7. The other vocabulary words are listed on pages 22 and 23.

Library and Archives Canada Cataloguing in Publication

Title: Little stars ballet / Taylor Farley.
Other titles: Ballet
Names: Farley, Taylor, author.
Description: Series statement: Little stars | "A Crabtree seedlings book". | Includes index. |
  Previously published in electronic format by Blue Door Education in 2020.
Identifiers: Canadiana 20200378848 | ISBN 9781427129734 (hardcover) | ISBN 9781427129918 (softcover)
Subjects: LCSH: Ballet—Juvenile literature.
Classification: LCC GV1787.5 .F37 2021 | DDC j792.8—dc23

Library of Congress Cataloging-in-Publication Data

Names: Farley, Taylor, author.
Title: Little stars ballet / Taylor Farley.
Description: New York, NY : Crabtree Publishing Company, [2021] | Series: Little stars: a Crabtree seedlings book | Includes index.
Identifiers: LCCN 2020049317 | ISBN 9781427129734 (hardcover) | ISBN 9781427129918 (paperback)
Subjects: LCSH: Ballet--Juvenile literature.
Classification: LCC GV1787.5 .F37 2021 | DDC 792.8--dc23
LC record available at https://lccn.loc.gov/2020049317

Crabtree Publishing Company

www.crabtreebooks.com   1–800–387–7650

e-book ISBN 978-0-997240-15-3

Print book version produced jointly with Blue Door Education in 2021

Written by Taylor Farley
Production coordinator and Prepress technician: Samara Parent
Print coordinator: Katherine Berti

Printed in the U.S.A./012021/CG20201102

Photo credits: Cover © Samuel Borges Photography; pages 2-3 © Satyrenko; pages 4-5 © Samuel Borges Photography; pages 6-7 © JoHo; page 9 © Sean Nel; pages 10-15 © D.J.McGee; pages 17 and 19 © Master1305; page 21 © Carlush. All photos and illustrations from Shutterstock.com

Published in Canada
Crabtree Publishing
616 Welland Ave.
St. Catharines, Ontario
L2M 5V6

Published in the United States
Crabtree Publishing
347 Fifth Ave.
Suite 1402-145
New York, NY 10016

Published in the United Kingdom
Crabtree Publishing
Maritime House
Basin Road North, Hove
BN41 1WR

Published in Australia
Crabtree Publishing
Unit 3 – 5 Currumbin Court
Capalaba
QLD 4157